THOMAS *Jefferson*

THOMAS *Jefferson*

OUR THIRD PRESIDENT

By Elizabeth Sirimarco

SPIRIT
of America™

The Child's World®, Inc.
Chanhassen, Minnesota

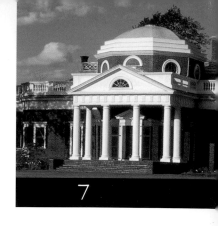

7

THOMAS *Jefferson*

Published in the United States of America by The Child's World®, Inc.
PO Box 326 • Chanhassen, MN 55317-0326 • 800-599-READ • www.childsworld.com

Acknowledgments

The Creative Spark: Mary Francis-DeMarois, Project Director; Elizabeth Sirimarco Budd, Series Editor; Robert Court, Design and Art Direction; Janine Graham, Page Layout; Jennifer Moyers, Production

The Child's World®, Inc.: Mary Berendes, Publishing Director; Red Line Editorial, Fact Research; Cindy Klingel, Curriculum Advisor; Robert Noyed, Historical Advisor

Photos

Cover: White House Collection, courtesy White House Historical Association; Adams National Historical Park: 35; Courtesy of the Architect of the Capitol (painting located on the first floor in the north corridor of the Senate wing at the Capitol): 24; Bettmann/Corbis: 27, 29; © Francis G. Mayer/ Corbis: 10; Independence National Historical Park: 6, 14, 18; Kevin Davidson: 23; The Library of Congress Collection: 9, 12, 15, 19, 20, 21, 22, 26, 28, 32, 35; Monticello/Thomas Jefferson Memorial Foundation, Inc.: 7, 33; Photodisc: 13; Stock Montage: 16, 30

Registration

Library of Congress Cataloging-in-Publication Data
Sirimarco, Elizabeth, 1966–
     Thomas Jefferson : our third president / by Elizabeth Sirimarco.
          p. cm.
     Includes bibliographical references and index.
     ISBN 1-56766-841-0 (lib. bdg. : alk. paper)
     1. Jefferson, Thomas, 1743–1826—Juvenile literature. 2. Presidents—United States—Biography—
Juvenile literature. [1. Jefferson, Thomas, 1743–1826. 2. Presidents.] I. Title.
E332.79 .S58 2001
973.4'6'092—dc21
                                                                        00-010568

10   13   27

Contents

Chapter ONE

The Path to Glory

Thomas Jefferson was the third president of the United States. Before he was elected to the country's most important office, he contributed his skill and intelligence to the nation in many other ways.

ALL HIS LIFE, NO MATTER WHERE HE TRAVELED, Thomas Jefferson longed for the Virginia countryside. He was born there on April 13, 1743, in Albemarle County. His family owned a tobacco **plantation.** This vast farm stretched across more than a thousand **acres** on the edge of wilderness, just east of the Blue Ridge Mountains. He would live in other places during his life, but it was always this wild and beautiful land that Jefferson called home.

As a young man, Jefferson dreamed of building a home on his family's land. He loved studying **architecture** and planned to design the home himself. He pictured it in a favorite spot where he often played as a child, a beautiful place high atop a hill. At age 27, he laid

Monticello, shown at left, is just outside the town of Charlottesville, Virginia. The sketch below, by Jefferson's own hand, depicts early ideas for the main house at Monticello.

the first bricks on that very site. He called his new home Monticello (mon-tee-CHEL-o), a word that means "little mountain" in Italian.

Two years later, in 1772, Jefferson married Martha Wayles Skelton. The young couple began their life together at Monticello. It was just a one-room cabin at the time, but he had plans to make it much bigger. He would grow colorful, lush gardens and plant fruit trees and grapevines. Jefferson hoped that one day it would be among the loveliest homes in all of Virginia.

From that time on, Monticello was Jefferson's favorite place in the world. He filled it with the things he loved best: his family, his books, beautiful music, and close friends. He spent many hours reading each day and loved to study science and nature. Sometimes he and Mrs. Jefferson read to each other. Other times, they performed duets, with Martha playing the **harpsichord** and Thomas playing the violin.

Although Monticello was the only place in the world that Jefferson truly wanted to be, he often had to leave. After all, he was one of America's founding fathers, the men who helped build the United States of America.

In 1776, the 13 American colonies were at war against powerful Great Britain. The American **Revolution** had been going on for one year. Jefferson was just 33 years old, but already he was known as an intelligent man and an excellent writer. During the Revolution, leaders from each colony were elected to the **Continental Congress.** Jefferson was among these men, and he traveled to Philadelphia to meet with **delegates** from other colonies.

Congress named Jefferson to a **committee** charged with writing an important **document.**

Benjamin Franklin, John Adams, and Thomas Jefferson (left to right) were all members of the five-man committee chosen to create the Declaration of Independence. As Jefferson wrote the first draft, he asked the other members for their suggestions.

It would tell the world that Americans no longer accepted Great Britain's rule. It would declare America's independence. Other committee members recognized Jefferson's talent as a writer, and they asked him to create the document.

It took Jefferson about two weeks to write the first **draft** of what became known as the **Declaration of Independence.** During that brief time, he composed some of the most important words ever written. He thought a great deal about what the draft should say.

Sometimes he got up from his desk to play the violin. He took short breaks to drink a cup of tea. Finally, he finished his work. "We hold these truths to be self-evident, that all men are created equal," wrote Jefferson. These words were at the heart of the Declaration and of what Jefferson believed. He hoped they would be the foundation of a great new country.

Jefferson's ideas helped build what the United States strives to be—a **democracy** where the people participate in their government.

Although Jefferson wrote the Declaration of Independence, Congress made several changes to it before all the states agreed to it on July 4th, 1776.

In all the important positions he held, Jefferson never lost sight of this goal.

The Revolution ended in 1781, and the United States had won its independence. Now came the work of building a new nation. The country needed all of its brightest men, and Jefferson was one of them. In the years that followed, his skill and intellect would help him become one of the most important leaders in American history. He was a man with the ability to **inspire** others, a man who never let go of his belief that the nation must be built on a foundation of liberty.

Jefferson's wife died in 1782. To mend his broken heart, he devoted all of his energy to the good of the country. He continued in his post as a member of the Continental Congress. Then he was named **minister** to France. He lived in France for five years. When he returned to Monticello in 1789, Jefferson learned there was a new job waiting for him. President George Washington asked him to be the **secretary of state.** Secretary Jefferson was now in charge of the new nation's relationships with foreign countries, and he was on his way to the capital city.

THOMAS JEFFERSON wrote the Declaration of Independence in 1776. More than half a million Americans were slaves at that time. This means one-fifth of the population was owned by other Americans. What did Jefferson mean when he wrote, "all men are created equal"? Why were some people equal, and others were not?

Jefferson believed slavery was wrong. He tried to create laws to stop it. He even wrote about it in the first draft of the Declaration of Independence. He wrote that slavery was a "cruel war against human nature itself." Unfortunately, other leaders took these words out. They did not want to make American slave owners angry.

"Nothing," wrote Jefferson, "is more certainly written in the book of fate, than that these people are to be free."

Yet Thomas Jefferson owned slaves all of his life. He inherited them from his father and from his wife's father. Many historians believe that he may even have had children with one of his slaves, a woman named Sally Hemmings. Although he owned more than 100 slaves in his lifetime, he only set five of them free. How could he keep them if he believed slavery was wrong? If some of these people were his own children, how could he enslave them?

There is no easy way to answer this question. Things were different then. Neither women nor blacks were considered the equals of white men. Jefferson followed the traditions of his family. His ideas were like those of many other Americans at that time in history. He also worried about what his slaves would do if they were free. How could they make enough money to live? How would white people treat them?

Jefferson depended on his slaves, too. They helped him build Monticello. They tended his garden and cooked for him. They kept his house. They grew crops in his fields. They did all these things without ever being paid. Slave owners would have had a hard time finding white people to do all of these things. If Jefferson freed his slaves, life at Monticello would have been very different.

Some people believe that Jefferson should have freed his slaves to prove that he thought slavery was wrong. He should have set an example for other slave owners. No one knows why he never did. Perhaps his words and ideas helped future Americans fight slavery and injustice. Today the Declaration of Independence is true for every American, not just a chosen few.

Chapter TWO

American Leader

Alexander Hamilton helped create the U.S. Constitution, but Jefferson did not believe that he truly understood its purpose.

EVEN IN THOMAS JEFFERSON'S DAY, LEADERS did not always agree with each other. Alexander Hamilton was the secretary of treasury. He was in charge of the country's **finances.** Jefferson and Hamilton were two of President Washington's most important assistants, but they disagreed about many things.

Jefferson still believed in the ideas of the American Revolution. In England, only rich, powerful men could participate in the government. Soldiers had fought in the Revolution so that *all* American citizens could have that right. Then the founding fathers wrote the **Constitution** to ensure it.

Unfortunately, Jefferson and the other founding fathers believed that only white men had these rights. Men of other races and women

Washington (at right) with three members of his cabinet (left to right): Henry Knox, Thomas Jefferson, and Alexander Hamilton. A president's cabinet helps make important decisions for the country, but the feud between Hamilton and Jefferson made it difficult for them to work together.

were not included in their definition of the word "citizen." Black men could not vote until 1870, and women could not vote until 1920. Still, it was revolutionary just to give these rights to all white men, regardless of whether they were rich or educated.

While Jefferson firmly believed in the rights promised by the Constitution, Hamilton did not think all men were capable of making serious decisions. He believed that a few powerful, educated leaders should take charge instead.

To Jefferson, Hamilton's idea of government sounded too much like that of Great Britain. It sounded like a monarchy, a country led by a king or queen. "Sometimes it is said that man cannot be trusted with the government of himself," Jefferson once said. "Can he, then, be trusted with the government of others? Or have we found angels in the forms of kings to govern him?"

The disputes between Jefferson and Hamilton gave birth to the nation's first **political parties.** Some leaders liked Jefferson's ideas, and these men joined together and called themselves

A 1789 political cartoon depicts Federalists and Republicans doing battle in Congress. Jefferson and Alexander Hamilton are said to be the founders of the nation's first political parties.

Republicans (also called the Democratic-Republicans). Others took Hamilton's side. These men called themselves **Federalists.** Just like today, the political parties struggled to help people who shared their ideas win elections. If there were more Republicans in office, they would be more likely to get their way. The same was true for the Federalists.

In 1792, Americans elected Washington—who did not join forces with either the Republicans or the Federalists—for a second **term of office.** Jefferson had already tried to retire twice. He wanted to return to a quiet life at Monticello, away from **politics.** But each time Jefferson tried to leave, President Washington asked him to stay. In 1793, at the age of 50, Jefferson finally quit, leaving "the hated occupation of politics."

Back at Monticello, Jefferson invented machines to help him do his work. He also studied nature and geography. He drew plans to improve Monticello, and he worked on his farm. He rarely thought about politics. But as the next election drew near, Washington said he would not run for a third term. The Republican leaders thought Jefferson might

17

John Adams was George Washington's vice president before he won the election of 1796. He became the second president of the United States.

be able to win the election. They asked him to run, but Jefferson said he would not. Could they change his mind?

Many people asked, but Jefferson always refused. His friends would not give up, and they named Jefferson as their **candidate.** Before he knew it, Jefferson was in a race for the presidency. His closest competitor was his longtime friend, the **patriot** John Adams.

Adams won the election, and Jefferson came in second. In those days, the second-place candidate became the vice president. Even though Adams was a Federalist, Jefferson hoped they could cooperate. He accepted the post of vice president and left Monticello to live in Philadelphia, the capital city at the time.

The Federalists and the Republicans argued throughout the next four years. Adams and Jefferson shared few goals. Jefferson worried that a few select people would run the country one day.

The next election was coming, and it was time for the Republicans to find a candidate. Only Jefferson seemed to have a chance. This time, he wanted to run for office. Perhaps he could help steer the nation back on course.

THOMAS JEFFERSON ALWAYS CONSIDERED HIMSELF A SCIENTIST FIRST, then a farmer, and finally a politician. "Nature intended me for the tranquil pursuits of science by [making] them my supreme delight," he once wrote. "But the enormities of the times in which I have lived … forced me to take a part in … them."

Jefferson was among Virginia's largest planters and believed that the growing of crops was an important science. He studied it with great interest and introduced many new plants to the United States. In fact, when Jefferson returned from France in 1789, he brought with him grapevines, rice, apricots, olive trees, and a variety of different seeds to plant on the grounds at Monticello. He also exchanged advice and seeds with other farmers who shared his love for the land.

Jefferson found a way to combine his interest in farming and his passion for science and invention by designing his own farm machinery. He and his son-in-law worked together to invent an iron plow that could work on steep hillsides. The drawing below is Jefferson's own sketch for the machine. He always used detailed math calculations to design his machinery, which made it easier to copy and improve his inventions later.

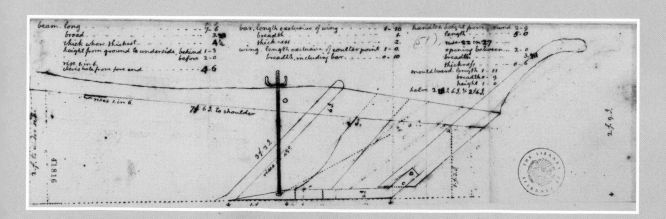

Chapter THREE

In Command

Thoughtful, shy Thomas Jefferson never wanted to be the president, but Americans knew he would take the job seriously.

ON MARCH 4, 1801, 57-YEAR-OLD THOMAS Jefferson became the third president of the United States. The election of 1800 had been difficult. After all the votes were counted, there was a tie. Jefferson and Aaron Burr both received 73 **electoral votes.** According to the Constitution, the House of Representatives had to decide who would be president.

Unfortunately, the House could not make a decision. There were 16 states, and each had one House vote. A candidate needed at least nine votes to win. The House voted 35 times, and each time, Jefferson received only eight votes.

Finally, Alexander Hamilton stepped in. He never liked Jefferson, but he didn't trust Aaron Burr at all. He believed Jefferson

would be a better choice for the country. "Jefferson is to be preferred," he wrote to one House representative, "he is by far not so dangerous a man." Finally, on the 36th ballot, Jefferson received 10 votes. Jefferson's rival had helped him win. Aaron Burr became the vice president.

President Jefferson's **inauguration** was the first to take place in Washington, D.C. He walked to the ceremony and wore simple clothing. In his quiet voice, he gave a speech

Jefferson was the first president to be inaugurated in Washington, D.C., the new capital city. At the time, the capital was little more than a small town. Construction of the city had begun early in President Washington's first term of office, only a decade before. The president's mansion, later called the White House, was still unfinished. It sat in the midst of a wild, forested landscape.

Aaron Burr and Thomas Jefferson received an equal number of votes in the election of 1800. Burr became the vice president when the House of Representatives elected Jefferson president.

that promised the country a new spirit of cooperation. "We are all Republicans, we are all Federalists," said Jefferson.

Soon after he became president, Jefferson learned about a secret agreement between France and Spain. It involved the Louisiana **territory.** Spain and France had both controlled the territory in the past, but things had begun to change. The French ruler, Napoleon, recently had won many battles in Europe, and France had become very powerful. In 1800, French leaders had forced Spain into making an agreement. Spain now had to give the Louisiana territory to France.

The Mississippi River was a vital part of the territory because land travel was difficult on both sides of the river. The United States used the river to transport both people and goods across the continent and to the sea. U.S. **trade** would be in trouble without the use of the Mississippi. The president feared that France might stop American ships from traveling on the river.

Jefferson thought hard. How could he save this important piece of land? Could he offer to buy it from France?

In 1803, Jefferson asked the minister to France, Robert Livingston, to **negotiate** an agreement. Congress said he could offer France $2 million to purchase part of the territory, including the city of New Orleans. This would secure the right for Americans to travel on the Mississippi. Jefferson's friend, James Monroe,

The Louisiana territory covered more than 800,000 square miles, stretching from the Mississippi River all the way to the Rocky Mountains. In the south, it began at the city of New Orleans and ran northwest to what are now the states of Minnesota, North Dakota, and Montana.

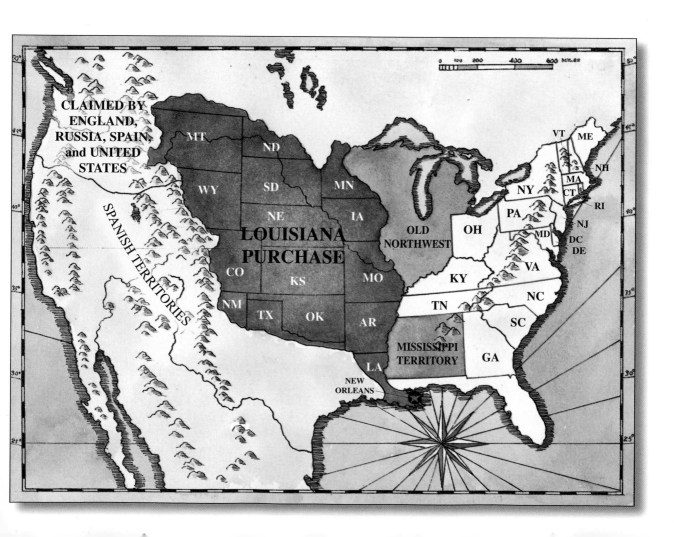

Americans James Monroe (center) and Robert Livingston (left) negotiated the Louisiana Purchase with the French foreign minister, Charles Talleyrand.

was sent to France to help. Monroe made the slow trip across the Atlantic Ocean while Livingston began talks with the French leaders.

At first, the French refused to agree. But then they asked how much the United States would pay for the land. French armies were fighting wars across Europe, and warfare was expensive. The French needed money badly. In addition, French leaders were simply too busy to worry about their land in America.

In April, Monroe arrived in France. The two countries made an agreement by the 29th of the month. The United States would pay France $15 million for the entire territory—about four cents an acre. They signed a **treaty** the next day. This agreement became known as the Louisiana Purchase. Now both the Mississippi and the Missouri rivers were inside U.S. borders. In one day, the country had doubled in size.

Livingston and Monroe wrote Jefferson a letter to tell him the good news, but it took a long time to reach him. A ship had to carry it from France, across the Atlantic Ocean. By the time it reached Washington, it was July 3. Jefferson was thrilled by the news. Newspapers told the public on a very special day: the fourth of July.

The Louisiana Purchase was a big success. President Jefferson was planning another exciting project, too. One of his assistants was a man named Meriwether Lewis. Mr. Lewis knew a lot about the American wilderness. The two men often talked about the continent's natural treasures. Wouldn't it be wonderful to learn about all the plants and animals that lived in the Louisiana territory —and even farther west than that?

Jefferson and Lewis began to plan an **expedition.** Lewis told the president about a skilled soldier named William Clark, who would be a good partner on the difficult journey. Lewis and Clark traveled up the Mississippi River to St. Louis. From there, they would begin their journey. Thirty soldiers and 10 scientists traveled with them. They left St. Louis on May 14, 1804, traveling slowly up the Missouri River. When they arrived in what is now North Dakota, they set out on foot toward the Pacific Ocean.

Meriwether Lewis studied mapmaking, botany, and zoology before he set out on his expedition with William Clark. He even received medical advice from a doctor so that he would be prepared for emergencies.

About 18 months later, the expedition reached the Pacific Ocean. On their journey, the team found 178 plant species and 122 animals that only Native Americans had ever seen before. They also learned about the continent's geography.

Everyone was proud of the Louisiana Purchase, and the Lewis and Clark expedition sparked Americans' interest in the vast continent they inhabited. The American people could thank President Jefferson for these achievements.

A Shoshone Indian woman named Sacagawea joined the Lewis and Clark expedition six months after they left St. Louis. She helped the American men communicate with Native Americans they met along the way.

Chapter FOUR

A Second Term

In the 1804 presidential election, Jefferson received a greater majority of votes than any other candidate would in that century.

IN 1804, IT WAS TIME TO VOTE AGAIN, AND Americans still wanted Thomas Jefferson to be their president. That year, 14 out of 16 states voted for him. George Clinton became his second vice president.

At the inauguration in 1805, President Jefferson spoke about the previous four years, and then he talked about plans for the future. He hoped to build new roads to the West and canals to connect the land's biggest rivers. These improvements would make it easier to transport goods to people across the continent.

Although his inauguration promised great things, Jefferson's next four years would be more difficult than his first term had been. There would be problems both at home and with foreign countries.

Aaron Burr was no longer the vice president, and he was angry. He believed the United States and its leaders had turned on him. Burr began plotting to hurt the United States. First, he secretly offered to help Great Britain take over the Louisiana territory. The British ignored him, but Burr didn't give up. He went to Louisiana anyway, hoping to start a **rebellion** himself.

In 1804, Aaron Burr challenged his long-time enemy, Alexander Hamilton, to a duel. He blamed Hamilton for ruining his political career. Burr shot and killed Hamilton on July 11.

Jefferson received a letter about the plot in February of 1806. He talked about the problem with his **cabinet.** Then he received more information, blaming Burr for the whole scheme. In 1807, Burr was arrested for **treason.** The court found him innocent, but no one trusted him anymore. The man who had once been the vice president had to leave American politics forever.

While President Jefferson was in office, the British began to stop American ships at sea and search them for English deserters.

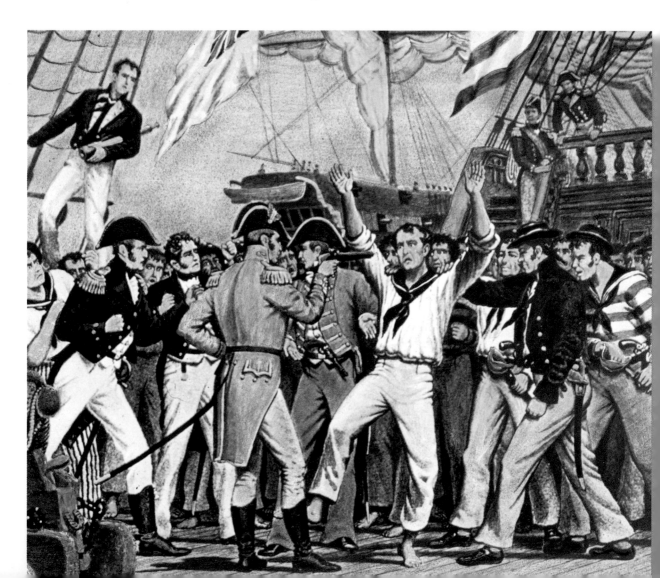

Problems were brewing with Great Britain, too. A British warship called the *Leopard* fired on an American **frigate,** the *Chesapeake.* The Commander of the *Leopard* had demanded permission to search the *Chesapeake.* He wanted to see if there were any British **deserters** on board. When the Americans refused, the British fired a cannon three times at the *Chesapeake.* In the fighting, 18 American sailors were wounded, and three died. After the Americans surrendered, the British captured four sailors. Three of these men were American citizens.

Americans were furious. They even wanted to go to war, but Jefferson wanted peace. He thought it was better to demand an apology from Britain and then banish their ships from American waters.

Unfortunately, British rulers refused to apologize. Jefferson asked Congress for help. In 1807, the members of Congress voted for an **embargo,** which stopped American ships from transporting goods to England.

Jefferson called for the embargo because he wanted to hurt Great Britain. The British used many American products, such as lumber,

A British political cartoon depicts Jefferson explaining the embargo to unhappy American citizens.

livestock, cotton, and tobacco. Jefferson thought if Americans took these things away, the British would apologize to get them back again.

Jefferson's plan didn't work. Americans did not use enough of the crops they grew. Grains and other goods spoiled in storage before they could be sold, and farmers lost a lot of money. Sailors and shipbuilders also lost their jobs because American trade ships were no longer sailing across the

32

Atlantic. Even worse, **smugglers** were sneaking U.S. goods to England.

The embargo made Jefferson's final year as president difficult, but many Americans wanted him to run for a third term. Jefferson reminded his supporters that President Washington had refused a third term. Both Washington and Jefferson believed that the leadership of the U.S. government should change often so that no person or group could gain too much power. Today no president can serve more than two terms.

Congress finally passed a bill to stop the embargo. Jefferson signed it on March 1, 1809, only three days before he would leave the presidency forever.

Before Jefferson left Washington, he went to the inaugural ball of James Madison, the new president. People noticed that Jefferson looked happy, but President Madison seemed nervous. Jefferson wasn't surprised. "I have got this burden off my shoulders," he said, "while he has got it on his."

This time, Jefferson would really retire. No one could convince him to return to politics. He would study and tend his gardens.

Interesting Facts

▸ James Madison's inaugural ball was the first dance Jefferson had attended since his wife's death.

▸ In 1815, Jefferson had to sell his entire library of 6,487 books to pay his debts. The government bought them and started the Library of Congress.

He would spend time with his grandchildren, teaching them about nature and reading to them. He would work hard to open the University of Virginia, the state's first public school. Thomas Jefferson was determined to spend the rest of his life in Virginia, with his family and friends. "Good wishes are all an old man has to offer his country or friends," he wrote in 1811. Until the day he died—July 4th, 1826—Jefferson never left Virginia again. Finally, he could truly call Monticello home.

The Thomas Jefferson Memorial Foundation owns Monticello today, and people can visit Jefferson's beautiful home in the Virginia hills.

THOMAS JEFFERSON AND JOHN ADAMS WERE CLOSE FRIENDS FOR MANY YEARS. The two patriots respected and admired each other during the Revolution, but they later began to have different ideas about the government. Jefferson won the election of 1800. After that, the two men did not speak for 12 years.

Finally, John Adams wrote to Jefferson on New Year's Day of 1812. He wished his old friend "many happy new years." Jefferson wrote back, and the two men continued to write long letters to each other for the rest of their lives.

In the summer of 1826, Jefferson was 83 years old. Adams was 90. Neither man was in good health, but both of them wanted to live—at least until the fourth of July. That day would mark a special anniversary. Fifty years before, the patriots had signed the Declaration of Independence. Both men wanted to celebrate the occasion.

On July 2, Jefferson became ill, and he slept most of the day. On the evening of July 3, he woke only long enough to ask, "Is it the fourth?" His doctor told him it would be soon.

At four o'clock in the afternoon on July 4, Adams said, "Thomas Jefferson survives." Adams died a moment later. He did not know that his close friend had died four hours earlier. Two of America's founding fathers, the nation's second and third presidents, had died on Independence Day—50 years after they had signed their names to the Declaration of Independence.

April 13, 1743 Thomas Jefferson is born in the Piedmont region of Virginia. His parents, Peter Jefferson and Jane Randolph Jefferson, own a large tobacco plantation.

1757 Peter Jefferson dies. At age 14, Thomas Jefferson inherits the family farm, 2,500 acres, and 30 slaves.

1760 Jefferson travels 150 miles to Williamsburg where he will attend the College of William and Mary. He begins studying law. He also studies French and continues to play the violin.

1767 Jefferson begins practicing law.

1768 Jefferson prepares the land to build Monticello.

1769 Jefferson becomes a member of the House of Burgesses, which is the Virginia state legislature. It is his first step toward a life of politics.

1770 Jefferson moves to Monticello.

1772 Jefferson marries Martha Wayles Skelton on January 1. Their first daughter, Martha (Patsy), is born on September 27.

1775 Jefferson is elected to the second Continental Congress in March. The American Revolution begins with the Battle of Lexington and Concord on April 19.

1776 Jefferson's mother dies on March 31. In June, he writes the Declaration of Independence. Members of Congress sign it on July 4. Congress designates "United States" as the nation's official name on September 9.

1778 The Jeffersons have a daughter named Mary and nickname her Polly.

1779 Jefferson is elected the governor of Virginia. He holds the position for two, one-year terms of office.

1781 The British surrender following their defeat at the Battle of Yorktown in Virginia on October 19.

1782 Martha Jefferson dies on September 6.

1783 Jefferson is elected as a Virginia representative to Congress.

1784 Jefferson is named the minister to France.

1789 Jefferson returns to the United States. He is named President Washington's secretary of state. He quickly begins to have difficulties with other government leaders, especially Alexander Hamilton.

1793 Jefferson resigns as secretary of state.

1796 Jefferson is elected vice president.

1800 The U.S. capital city is moved from Philadelphia to Washington, D.C. Jefferson and Aaron Burr tie in the presidential election.

1801 The House of Representatives votes for Jefferson as president. He is the first president inaugurated in the new capital city.

1803 President Jefferson asks Congress to pay for the Lewis and Clark expedition in January. In April, the United States purchases the Louisiana Territory for $15 million.

1804 The Lewis and Clark expedition departs in May. Alexander Hamilton is shot and killed in July. President Jefferson is reelected in November.

1805 President Jefferson is inaugurated for his second term.

1806 President Jefferson receives letters warning him that Aaron Burr is plotting to take over the Louisiana territory.

1807 Aaron Burr is captured near New Orleans in January. Burr is found innocent of treason and leaves for England. In June, the British warship *Leopard* attacks the *Chesapeake*. The United States begins an embargo against Great Britain in December. It closes American ports to all foreign trade.

1808 The embargo is a failure. Despite this problem, many people want President Jefferson to run for a third term. He refuses. James Madison is elected president on December 7.

1809 Jefferson signs an act to end the embargo on March 1. On March 4, he retires from public office and returns to Monticello. He will never leave the state of Virginia again.

1825 The University of Virginia, the state's first public school, opens on March 7. Jefferson is its founder.

July 4, 1826 Jefferson dies shortly after 12 noon. It is the 50th anniversary of the Declaration of Independence. He is 83 years old.

acres (AY-kerz)
Acres are units of measurement.
Land is measured in acres.

architecture (arr-kuh-TEK-chur)
Architecture is the science and art of
making buildings. Thomas Jefferson
studied architecture.

cabinet (KAB-eh-net)
A cabinet is a group of people who
offer advice to a president or ruler.
Thomas Jefferson was a member of
President Washington's cabinet.

candidate (KAN-duh-det)
A candidate is a person running
for office. The Republicans chose
Jefferson as their candidate for
president in the election of 1800.

committee (kuh-MIH-tee)
A committee is a group of people
appointed or elected to do something special. Thomas Jefferson was
appointed to the committee in
charge of writing the Declaration
of Independence.

Constitution (kon-stuh-TOO-shun)
A constitution is a set of basic
principles that govern a state,
country, or society. The U.S.
Constitution describes the way
the United States is governed.

**Continental Congress
(kon-tuh-NEN-tul KONG-gris)**
The Continental Congress was the
group of men who governed the
United States during and after the
Revolution. Thomas Jefferson was a
member of the Continental Congress.

**Declaration of Independence
(deh-kluh-RAY-shun OF in-dee-
PEN-dens)**
The Declaration of Independence
is a document that was written by
Thomas Jefferson in 1776. It
announced the independence of
the United States of America from
Great Britain.

delegates (DEL-uh-gitz)
Delegates are people who are elected
by others to take part in something.
Each colony sent delegates to the
Continental Congress.

democracy (dee-MOK-reh-see)
A democracy is a country in which
the government is run by the people
who live there. The United States is
a democracy.

deserters (dih-ZER-turz)
Deserters are people who leave something that they shouldn't leave, such as the military. The British searched American ships for sailors that they claimed had deserted their navy.

document (DOK-yuh-ment)
A document is a written or printed paper that gives people important information. The Declaration of Independence is a document.

draft (DRAFT)
A draft is one of the first versions of an important paper or document. Jefferson wrote the first draft of the Declaration of Independence.

electoral votes (ee-LEKT-uh-rul VOTZ)
Electoral votes are votes cast by representatives of the American public for the president and vice president. Each state chooses representatives who vote for a candidate in an election. These representatives vote according to what the majority of people in their state want.

embargo (em-BAR-go)
An embargo stops one country from selling its goods to another country. The United States began an embargo against England in 1807.

expedition (ek-speh-DISH-en)
An expedition is a journey taken for a special reason, such as exploring new lands or for scientific study. The Lewis and Clark Expedition reached the Pacific Ocean on November 7, 1805.

Federalists (FED-ur-ul-ists)
The Federalists were a political party in Jefferson's time that was similar to today's Republicans. Federalists believed that a few well-educated people should run the nation.

finances (FYE-nan-siz)
Finances are the money and income that a person, country, or company has. The secretary of treasury is in charge of the nation's finances.

frigate (FRIG-it)
A frigate is a fast, medium-sized warship. The *Chesapeake* was a frigate.

harpsichord (HARP-seh-kord)
A harpsichord is an instrument that has a keyboard like a piano. Martha Jefferson played the harpsichord.

inauguration (ih-nawg-yuh-RAY-shun)
An inauguration is the ceremony that takes place when a new president begins a term. Thomas Jefferson wore simple clothing to his inauguration.

inspire (in-SPYR)
If a person inspires others, he or she causes them to think or feel something strongly. Jefferson inspired people to believe in democracy.

minister (MIN-eh-stir)
A minister is a person who is in charge of one part of the government. The U.S. minister to France takes care of the relationship between the United States and France.

negotiate (neh-GO-she-ate)
If people negotiate, they talk things over and try to come to an agreement. The United States and France had to negotiate the Louisiana Purchase.

patriot (PAY-tree-ut)
A patriot was any of the American colonists who wanted independence from Britain. Thomas Jefferson, George Washington, and John Adams were all patriots.

plantation (plan-TAY-shun)
A plantation is a large farm. Plantations grow crops such as tobacco, sugarcane, or cotton.

political parties (puh-LIT-uh-kul PAR-teez)
Political parties are groups of people who share similar ideas about how to run a government. The first U.S. political parties were the Republicans and the Federalists.

politics (PAWL-uh-tiks)
Politics refers to the actions and practices of the government. Thomas Jefferson often claimed that he disliked politics.

rebellion (ree-BELL-yen)
A rebellion is a fight against one's government. Aaron Burr wanted to start a rebellion and separate the Louisiana territory from the United States.

Republicans (ree-PUB-lih-kunz)
Republicans were a political party in Jefferson's time that was similar to today's Democrats. Republicans of the time believed that the U.S. government should be run by the nation's people.

revolution (rev-uh-LOO-shun)
A revolution is something that causes a complete change in government. The American Revolution was a war fought between the United States and Great Britain.

**secretary of state
(SEK-ruh-tair-ee OF STAYT)**
The secretary of state is a close advisor to the president. He or she is involved with the nation's relations with other countries.

smugglers (SMUG-lerz)
Smugglers are people who illegally bring in or take out something from a country. During the embargo from 1807 to 1809, smugglers took U.S. goods to Britain.

term of office (TERM OF AW-fiss)
A term of office is the length of time a politician can keep his or her position by law. A U.S. president's term of office is four years.

territory (TAIR-uh-tor-ee)
A territory is a land or region, especially land that belongs to a government. The U.S. purchased the Louisiana territory from France in 1803.

trade (TRAYD)
Trade is the business of buying and selling things. The United States has trade with other countries.

treason (TREE-zun)
Treason is the act hurting one's country or helping its enemies. Aaron Burr was arrested for treason.

treaty (TREE-tee)
A treaty is a formal agreement between two countries. France and the United States signed a treaty for the Louisiana Purchase on April 30, 1803.

Our PRESIDENTS

President	Birthplace	Life Span	Presidency	Political Party	First Lady
George Washington	Virginia	1732–1799	1789–1797	None	Martha Dandridge Custis Washington
John Adams	Massachusetts	1735–1826	1797–1801	Federalist	Abigail Smith Adams
Thomas Jefferson	Virginia	1743–1826	1801–1809	Democratic-Republican	widower
James Madison	Virginia	1751–1836	1809–1817	Democratic Republican	Dolley Payne Todd Madison
James Monroe	Virginia	1758–1831	1817–1825	Democratic Republican	Elizabeth Kortright Monroe
John Quincy Adams	Massachusetts	1767–1848	1825–1829	Democratic-Republican	Louisa Johnson Adams
Andrew Jackson	South Carolina	1767–1845	1829–1837	Democrat	widower
Martin Van Buren	New York	1782–1862	1837–1841	Democrat	widower
William H. Harrison	Virginia	1773–1841	1841	Whig	Anna Symmes Harrison
John Tyler	Virginia	1790–1862	1841–1845	Whig	Letitia Christian Tyler / Julia Gardiner Tyler
James K. Polk	North Carolina	1795–1849	1845–1849	Democrat	Sarah Childress Polk

Our PRESIDENTS

President	Birthplace	Life Span	Presidency	Political Party	First Lady
Zachary Taylor	Virginia	1784–1850	1849–1850	Whig	Margaret Mackall Smith Taylor
Millard Fillmore	New York	1800–1874	1850–1853	Whig	Abigail Powers Fillmore
Franklin Pierce	New Hampshire	1804–1869	1853–1857	Democrat	Jane Means Appleton Pierce
James Buchanan	Pennsylvania	1791–1868	1857–1861	Democrat	never married
Abraham Lincoln	Kentucky	1809–1865	1861–1865	Republican	Mary Todd Lincoln
Andrew Johnson	North Carolina	1808–1875	1865–1869	Democrat	Eliza McCardle Johnson
Ulysses S. Grant	Ohio	1822–1885	1869–1877	Republican	Julia Dent Grant
Rutherford B. Hayes	Ohio	1822–1893	1877–1881	Republican	Lucy Webb Hayes
James A. Garfield	Ohio	1831–1881	1881	Republican	Lucretia Rudolph Garfield
Chester A. Arthur	Vermont	1829–1886	1881–1885	Republican	widower
Grover Cleveland	New Jersey	1837–1908	1885–1889	Democrat	Frances Folsom Cleveland

President	Birthplace	Life Span	Presidency	Political Party	First Lady
Benjamin Harrison	Ohio	1833–1901	1889–1893	Republican	Caroline Scott Harrison
Grover Cleveland	New Jersey	1837–1908	1893–1897	Democrat	Frances Folsom Cleveland
William McKinley	Ohio	1843–1901	1897–1901	Republican	Ida Saxton McKinley
Theodore Roosevelt	New York	1858–1919	1901–1909	Republican	Edith Kermit Carow Roosevelt
William H. Taft	Ohio	1857–1930	1909–1913	Republican	Helen Herron Taft
Woodrow Wilson	Virginia	1856–1924	1913–1921	Democrat	Ellen L. Axson Wilson Edith Bolling Galt Wilson
Warren G. Harding	Ohio	1865–1923	1921–1923	Republican	Florence Kling De Wolfe Harding
Calvin Coolidge	Vermont	1872–1933	1923–1929	Republican	Grace Goodhue Coolidge
Herbert C. Hoover	Iowa	1874–1964	1929–1933	Republican	Lou Henry Hoover
Franklin D. Roosevelt	New York	1882–1945	1933–1945	Democrat	Anna Eleanor Roosevelt Roosevelt
Harry S. Truman	Missouri	1884–1972	1945–1953	Democrat	Elizabeth Wallace Truman

Our PRESIDENTS

President	Birthplace	Life Span	Presidency	Political Party	First Lady
Dwight D. Eisenhower	Texas	1890–1969	1953–1961	Republican	Mary "Mamie" Doud Eisenhower
John F. Kennedy	Massachusetts	1917–1963	1961–1963	Democrat	Jacqueline Bouvier Kennedy
Lyndon B. Johnson	Texas	1908–1973	1963–1969	Democrat	Claudia Alta Taylor Johnson
Richard M. Nixon	California	1913–1994	1969–1974	Republican	Thelma Catherine Ryan Nixon
Gerald Ford	Nebraska	1913–	1974–1977	Republican	Elizabeth "Betty" Bloomer Warren Ford
James Carter	Georgia	1924–	1977–1981	Democrat	Rosalynn Smith Carter
Ronald Reagan	Illinois	1911–	1981–1989	Republican	Nancy Davis Reagan
George Bush	Massachusetts	1924–	1989–1993	Republican	Barbara Pierce Bush
William Clinton	Arkansas	1946–	1993–2001	Democrat	Hillary Rodham Clinton
George W. Bush	Texas	1946–	2001–	Republican	Laura Welch Bush

Presidential FACTS

Qualifications
To run for president, a candidate must
- be at least 35 years old
- be a citizen who was born in the United States
- have lived in the United States for 14 years

Term of Office
A president's term of office is four years. No president can stay in office for more than two terms.

Election Date
The presidential election takes place every four years on the first Tuesday of November.

Inauguration Date
Presidents are inaugurated on January 20.

Oath of Office
I do solemnly swear I will faithfully execute the office of the President of the United States and will to the best of my ability preserve, protect, and defend the Constitution of the United States.

Write a Letter to the President
One of the best things about being a U.S. citizen is that Americans get to participate in their government. They can speak out if they feel government leaders aren't doing their jobs. They can also praise leaders who are going the extra mile. Do you have something you'd like the president to do? Should the president worry more about the environment and encourage people to recycle? Should the government spend more money on our schools? You can write a letter to the president to say how you feel!

1600 Pennsylvania Avenue
Washington, D.C. 20500

You can even send an e-mail to: president@whitehouse.gov

For Further INFORMATION

Internet Sites

Learn more about Thomas Jefferson's life:
http://gi.grolier.com/presidents/ea/bios/03pjeff.html

Learn more about the Declaration of Independence from the Library of Congress:
http://lcweb.loc.gov/exhibits/declara/declara1.html

Learn more about the Lewis and Clark expedition:
http://www.lewisclark.net/

Learn more about the Louisiana Purchase and take a trivia quiz:
http://members.tripod.com/~jtlawson/index.html

Visit Monticello: http://www.monticello.org/

Spend a day with Thomas Jefferson at Monticello:
http://www.monticello.org/jefferson/index.html

Find out how to visit the Jefferson Memorial in Washington, D.C.:
http://sc94.ameslab.gov/TOUR/jeffmem.html

More links to sites about Thomas Jefferson:
http://etext.virginia.edu/jefferson/quotations/jeffsite.htm

Learn more about all the presidents and visit the White House:
http://www.whitehouse.gov/WH/glimpse/presidents/html/presidents.html
http://www.thepresidency.org/presinfo.htm
http://www.americanpresidents.org/

Books

Barrett, Marvin. *Meet Thomas Jefferson.* New York: Random House, 1989.

Blumberg, Rhoda. *What's the Deal? Jefferson, Napoleon, and the Louisiana Purchase.* Washington, DC: The National Geographic Society, 1998.

Bober, Natalie S. *Thomas Jefferson: Man on a Mountain.* Aladdin Paperbacks, 1997.

Bohner, Charles. *Bold Journey: West with Lewis and Clark.* New York: Houghton Mifflin Company, 1990.

Young, Robert. *A Personal Tour of Monticello (How It Looked).* Minneapolis, MN: Lerner Publications Company, 1999.

Index